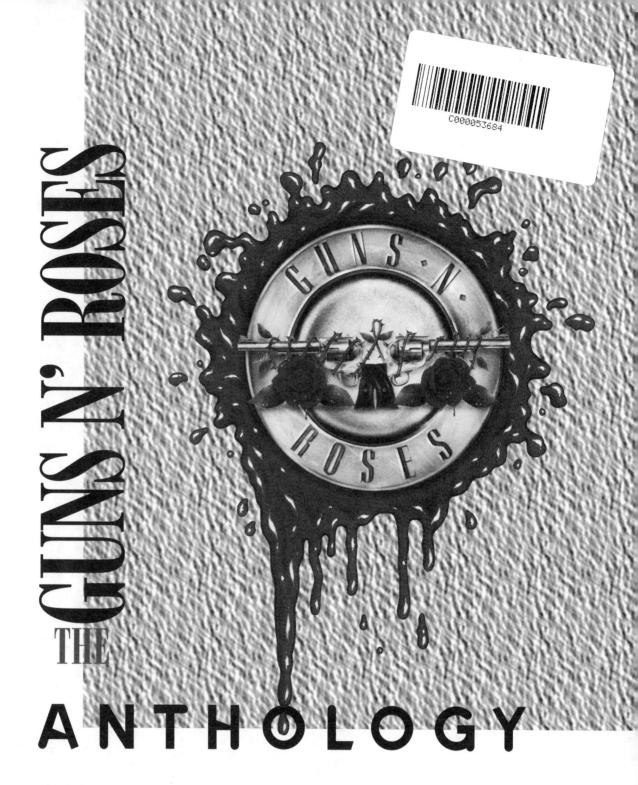

GUNS N' ROSES

THE

ANTHOLOGY

Management: Doug Goldstein/Big FD Entertainment, Inc.
Music Engraving: W.R. Music
Production: Daniel Rosenbaum/Rana Bernhardt
Art Direction: Rosemary Cappa-Jenkins/Art Brooks
Director of Music: Mark Phillips

59,-

Matt

Slash

Gilbey

T E

Photography: Gene Kirkland: Dizzy, Matt and Gilbey
Robert John: Axl, Slash and Duff

Duff

CON-TENTS

from **Appetite For Destruction**

4	Sweet Child O' Mine
14	Welcome To The Jungle
24	Mr. Brownstone
29	My Michelle
35	Nightrain
45	Paradise City
55	Rocket Queen
63	You're Crazy

from **G N' R Lies**

68	Patience
76	Used To Love Her

from **Use Your Illusion I**

80	November Rain
100	Bad Apples
107	Don't Cry (Original)
118	The Garden
128	Dead Horse

from **Use Your Illusion II**

138	Civil War
149	Yesterdays
153	Pretty Tied Up (The Perils Of Rock N' Roll Decadence)
161	Locomotive (Complicity)
177	Estranged
191	You Could Be Mine
207	Tablature Explanation/Notation Legend

Axl

Dizzy

SWEET CHILD O' MINE

Words and Music by
W. Axl Rose, Slash, Izzy Stradlin',
Duff "Rose" McKagan and Steven Adler

Whoa, oh,— oh, oh,—— sweet child o' mine.—

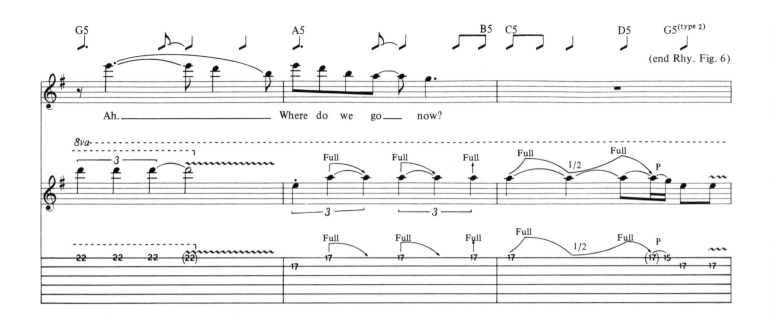

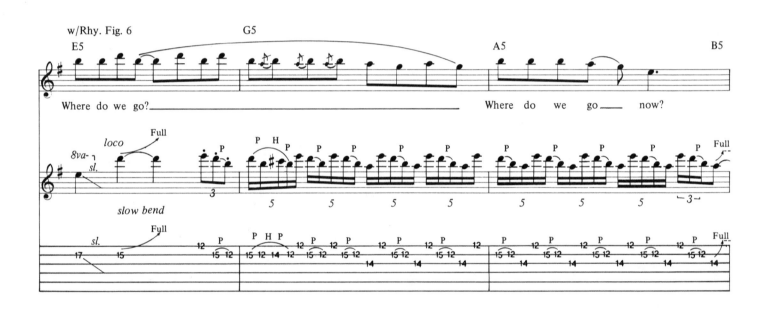

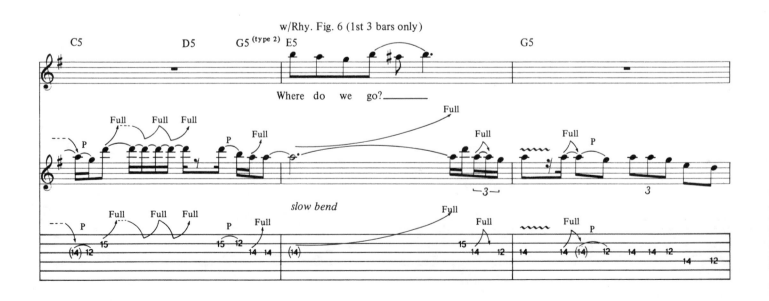

12

Additional Lyrics

2. She's got eyes of the bluest skies, as if they thought of rain.
   I hate to look into those eyes and see an ounce of pain.
   Her hair reminds me of a warm safe place where as a child I'd hide,
   And pray for the thunder and the rain to quietly pass me by. *(To Chorus)*

WELCOME TO THE JUNGLE

Words and Music by
W. Axl Rose, Slash, Izzy Stradlin',
Duff "Rose" McKagan and Steven Adler

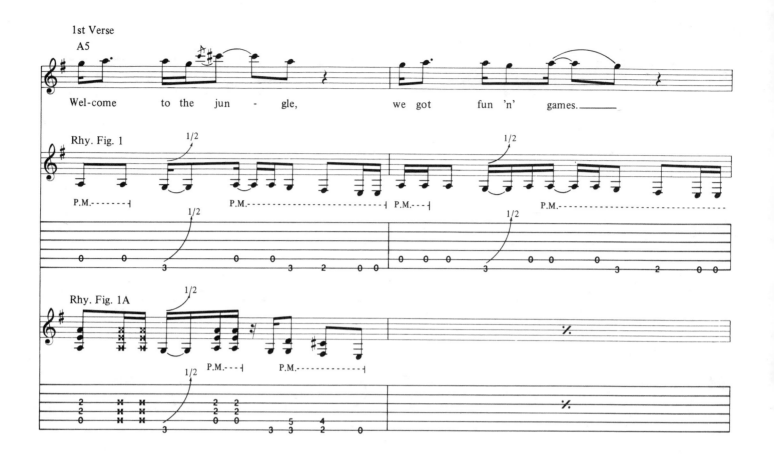

3rd Verse
w/Rhy. Figs. 1 & 1A
A5

Wel - come to the jun - gle, it gets worse here ev - 'ry day.___ You

learn to live___ like an an - i - mal,___ in the jun - gle where we play. If you got a

hun - ger for what you see,___ you'll take it e - ven - tu'l - ly. You can have an - y - thing you want,___ but you
w/Rhy. Fig. 2

bet - ter not take it from me.___ In the jun - gle, wel - come to the jun - gle. Watch it bring you to your
(Ah,_____ ah.)

MR. BROWNSTONE

Words and Music by
W. Axl Rose, Slash, Izzy Stradlin',
Duff "Rose" McKagan and Steven Adler

1st, 2nd Verses

N.C. (E5)   (A5)   (E5)

1. I get up a-round sev-en,   get out-ta bed a-round nine.   And
2. *See additional lyrics*

(Both gtrs.)

Rhy. Fig. 3

(A5)   ⌐3¬   (E5)

I don't wor-ry a-bout noth-in', no, 'cause wor-ry-in's a waste of my time.

(end Rhy. Fig. 3)

Chorus

G F G   C Bb C   D C D

We been danc-in' with Mis-ter Brown-stone. He's been knock-in'.

Rhy. Fig. 4   (end Rhy. Fig. 4)

2nd time to Coda I;
3rd time to Coda II

N.C.   N.C. (E5)

He won't leave me a-lone!   No, no, no. He won't leave me a-lone.

1/2   1/2   1/2   1/2

25

Now I get up a-round when-ev - er. I used to get up— on time. But

that old man,— he's a real muth-a-fuck-er, gon-na kick him on down the line._____ I

27

Coda II

w/Rhy. Fig. 1 *(2 times)* & 2

Stuck it in the mid - dle and I shot it in the mid - dle and it,

it drove me out - ta my mind.___

I should-'ve known bet - ter, said I wish I nev - er met her, said I,

I leave it all be - hind._____ Yow - sa!

Additional Lyrics

2. The show usually starts around seven.
   We go on stage around nine.
   Get on the bus around eleven,
   Sippin' a drink and feelin' fine. *(To Chorus)*

MY MICHELLE

Words and Music by
W. Axl Rose, Slash, Izzy Stradlin',
Duff "Rose" McKagan and Steven Adler

w/Riff A & Rhy. Fig. 2 *(both 1½ times)*

Riff B (Gtr. III)

w/Fill 2

Gtr. II

1st, 2nd, 3rd Verses

1. Your dad-dy works in por-no now tnat mom-my's not a-round. She

2.3. *See additional lyrics*

Rhy. Fig. 3 (both gtrs.)

slow release

P.M.

used to love her her-o-in but now she's un-der-ground. So you stay out late at night, and you

(end Rhy. Fig. 3)

sl.

long slide

w/Rhy. Fig. 3

do your coke for free Driv-in' your friends cra-zy with your life's in-san-i-ty.

(Both gtrs.)

Fill 2 (Gtr. I)

1½slow release

Additional Lyrics

2. Sowin' all your wild oats in another's luxuries.
   Yesterday was Tuesday, maybe Thursday you can sleep.
   But school starts much too early, and this hotel wasn't free.
   So party till your connection calls; honey, I'll return the key. *(To Chorus)*

3. Now you're clean and so discreet. I won't say a word.
   But most of all, this song is true, case you haven't heard.
   So come on and stop your cryin', 'cause we both know money burns.
   Honey, don't stop tryin' and you'll get what you deserve. *(To Chorus)*

NIGHTRAIN

Words and Music by
W. Axl Rose, Slash, Izzy Stradlin',
Duff "Rose" McKagan and Steven Adler

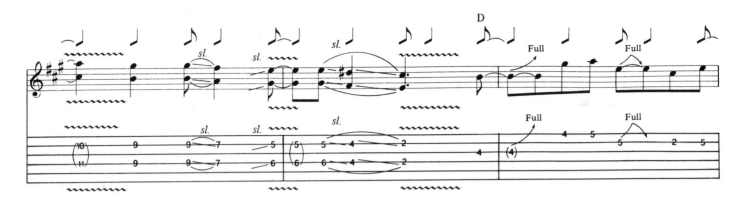

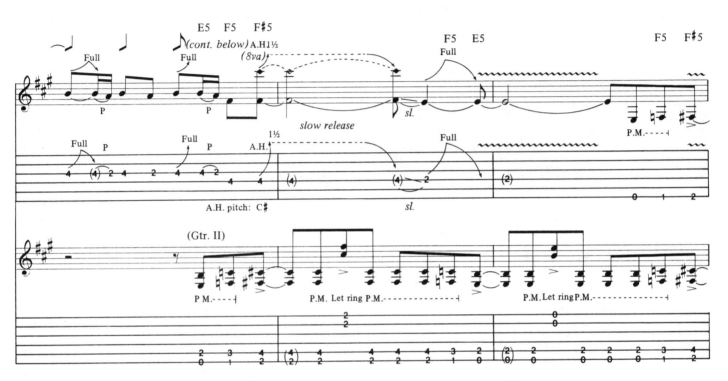

*See additional lyrics

Additional Lyrics

Outro Chorus:
Nightrain, bottom's up.
I'm on the nightrain, fill my cup.
I'm on the nightrain, whoa yeah!

I'm on the nightrain, love that stuff.
I'm on the nightrain, and I can never get enough.
Ridin' the nightrain, I guess I,
I guess, I guess, I guess I never learn.

On the nightrain, float me home.
Oh, I'm on the nightrain.
Ridin' the nightrain, never to return.

Nightrain.

PARADISE CITY

Words and Music by
W. Axl Rose, Slash, Izzy Stradlin',
Duff "Rose" McKagan and Steven Adler

1st, 2nd, 3rd, 4th Verses
w/Riff D (3rd, 4th times add Riff F)

1. Just a ur-chin liv-in' un-der the street.— I'm a ____ hard case that's tough to beat.— I'm your

2.3.4. *See additional lyrics*

Riff D

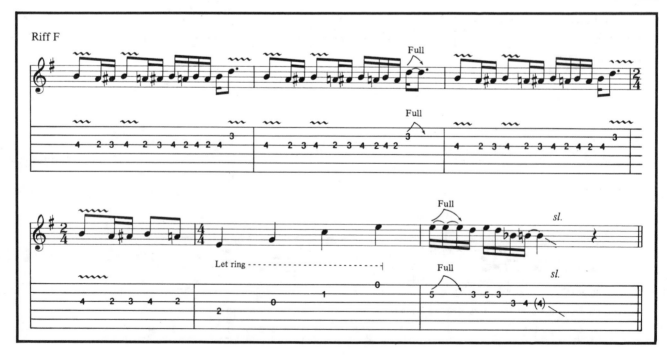

Riff F

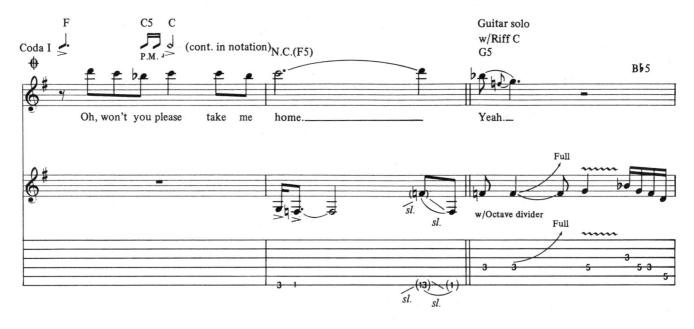
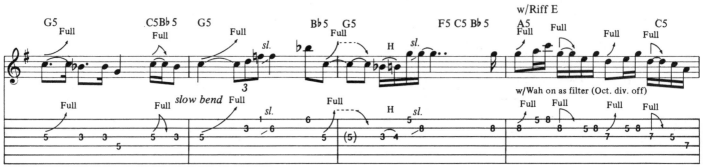
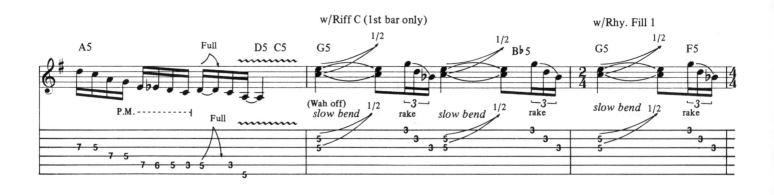
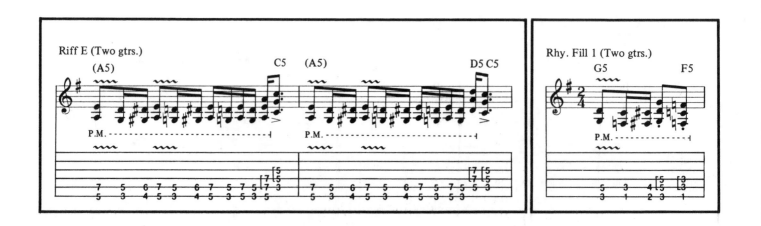

Oh, won't you please take me home,

home.

* Slow slide up middle 4 strings (off neck)   *As before

Double time ♩ = 208

Rhy.
Fig. 3

(end Rhy. Fig. 3)

w/Lead vocal ad lib (on Chorus) *(till notation returns)*
*w/Rhy. Fig. 3 *(9½ times)*
**G5

w/Octave divider

*Vary strumming rhythm at will.

** Use "type 2" till end.

51

Slower

Free time

Oh, won't you please take me home.

Additional Lyrics

2. Ragz to richez, or so they say.
Ya gotta keep pushin' for the fortune and fame.
It's all a gamble when it's just a game.
Ya treat it like a capital crime.
Everybody's doin' their time. *(To Chorus)*

3. Strapped in the chair of the city's gas chamber,
Why I'm here I can't quite remember.
The surgeon general says it's hazardous to breathe.
I'd have another cigarette but I can't see.
Tell me who ya gonna believe? *(To Chorus)*

4. Captain America's been torn a part.
Now he's a court jester with a broken heart.
He said, "Turn me around and take me back to the start."
I must be losin' my mind. "Are you blind?"
I've seen it all a million times. *(To Chorus)*

ROCKET QUEEN

Words and Music by
W. Axl Rose, Slash, Izzy Stradlin',
Duff "Rose" McKagan and Steven Adler

Here I am,—

60

YOU'RE CRAZY

Words and Music by
W. Axl Rose, Slash, Izzy Stradlin',
Duff "Rose" McKagan and Steven Adler

Additional Lyrics

2. Said where you goin'?
   What you gonna do?
   I been lookin' everywhere
   I been lookin' for you.
   You don't want my love, *(etc.)*

3. Say boy, where ya comin' from?
   Where'd ya get that point of view?
   When I was younger
   Said I knew someone like you.
   And they said you don't want my love, *(etc.)*

PATIENCE

Words and Music by
W. Axl Rose, Slash, Izzy Stradlin',
Duff "Rose" McKagan and Steven Adler

1. Shed a tear 'cause I'm miss-in' you,___ I'm still al-right___ to smile.___
2. *See additional lyrics*

70

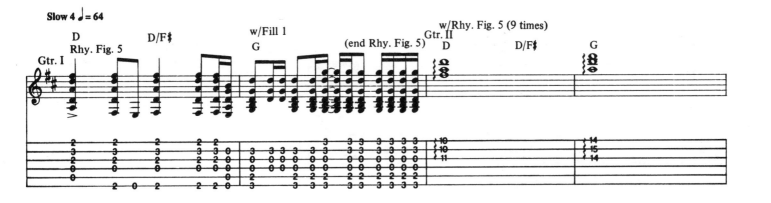

... lit - tle pa - tience, mm yeah,_____ mm __

yeah. _ Need a lit - tle pa - tience, yeah,_____ just a lit - tle

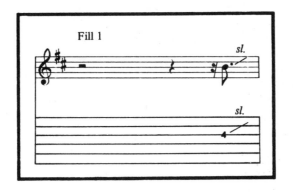

Additional Lyrics

2. I sit here on the stairs 'cause I'd rather be alone.
If I can't have you right now I'll wait, dear.
Sometimes I get so tense but I can't speed up the time.
But you know, love, there's one more thing to consider.

Said, woman, take it slow and things will be just fine.
You and I'll just use a little patience.
Said, sugar, take the time 'cause the lights are shining bright.
You and I've got what it takes to make it.
We won't fake it, ah, I'll never break it 'cause I can't take it. *(To Gtr. solo)*

USED TO LOVE HER

Words and Music by
W. Axl Rose, Slash, Izzy Stradlin',
Duff "Rose" McKagan and Steven Adler

*Sing 8va 3rd and 4th times.

Additional Lyrics

2. I used to love her, but I had to kill her.
   I used to love her, but I had to kill her.
   I knew I'd miss her so I had to keep her.
   She's buried right in my back yard.

3. I used to love her, but I had to kill her.
   I used to love her, but I had to kill her.
   She bitched so much she drove me nuts
   And now I'm happier this way.

4. *Repeat 1st Verse*

NOVEMBER RAIN

Words and Music by
W. Axl Rose

And it's hard to hold a can - dle in the cold No - vem - ber rain.

let ring- let ring- - - - - - - let ring- - - - - - - let ring- - - - - - - -

We've been through this such a long, long time just try - in' to kill the pain.

let ring- - - - -

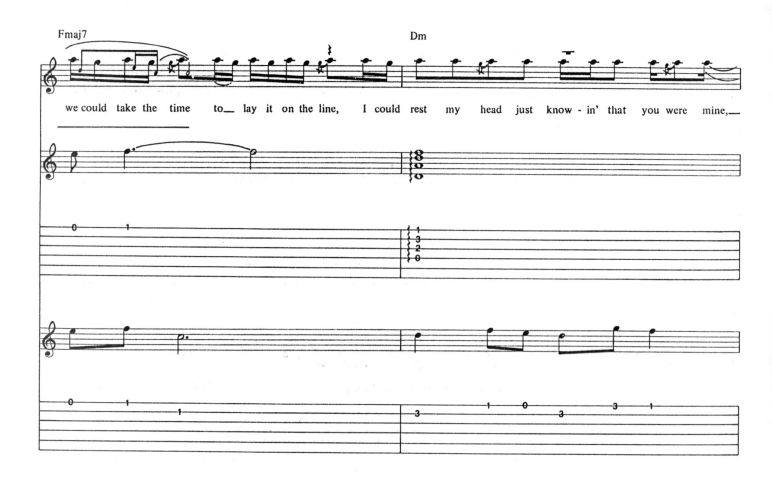

we could take the time to__ lay it on the line, I could rest my head just know - in' that you were mine,

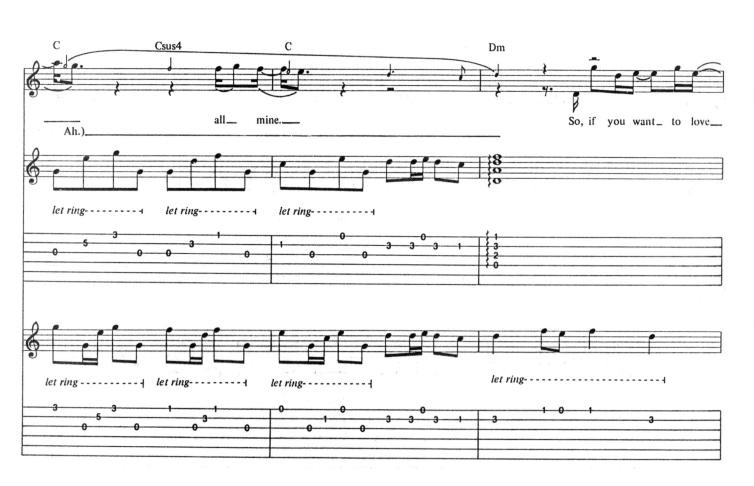

all__ mine.__

Ah.)

So, if you want__ to love__

let ring---------- let ring----------- let ring-----------

let ring----------- let ring----------- let ring----------- let ring-----------------------

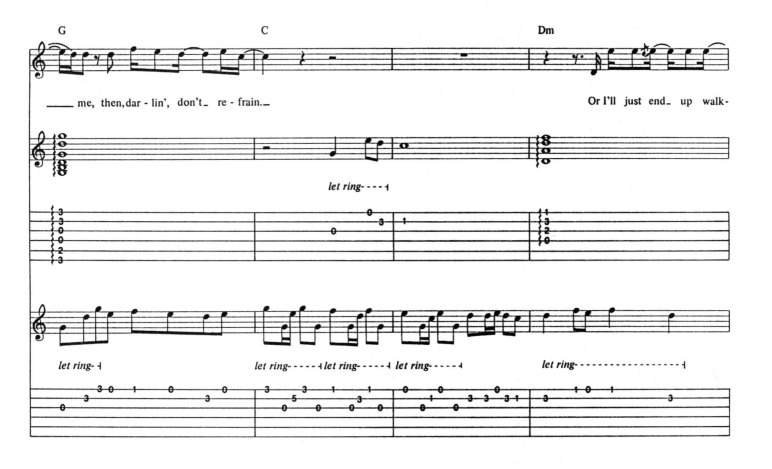

me, then, dar - lin', don't re - frain.___ Or I'll just end_ up walk-

in' in the cold No - vem - ber rain.___ Do you need_

(cont. in slashes)

would-n't time_ be out_ to charm___ you? Woh. _____

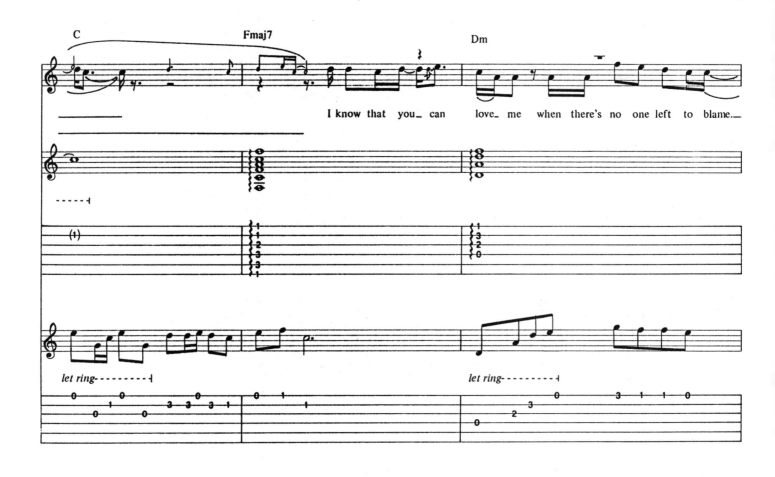

I know that you can love me when there's no one left to blame.

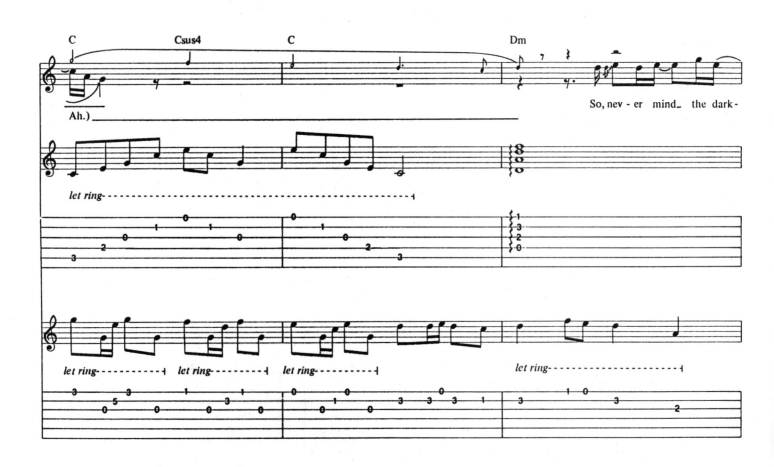

So, nev-er mind the dark-

ness. We still can find a way.

Nothin' lasts forever, even cold November rain.

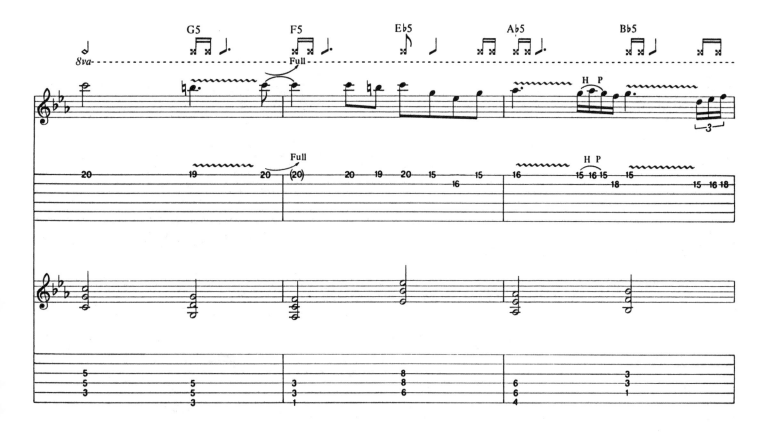

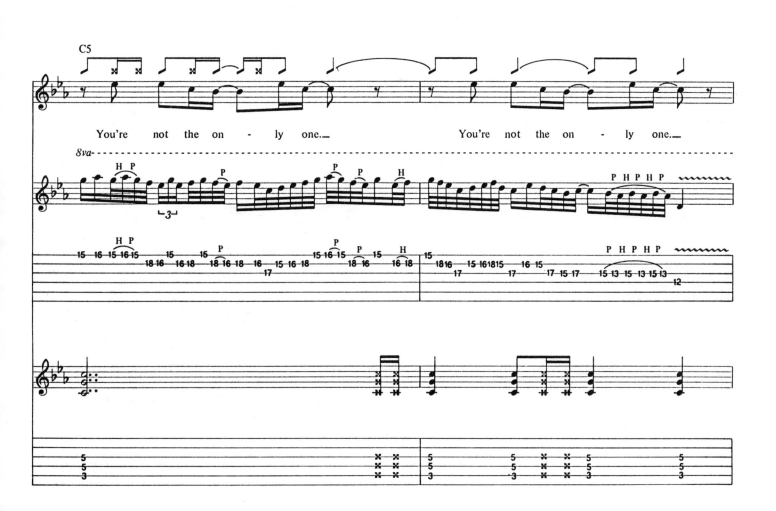

BAD APPLES

Words and Music by
Slash, Duff McKagan,
Izzy Stradlin' and W. Axl Rose

*Rhy. Gtr. II and Kybd. arr. for gtr. (Played w/ad lib rhythm variations throughout.)
**Rhy. Gtr. I and Bass arr. for gtr.

w/Rhy. Fig. 1A

Rhy. Fig. 2A   E5

head-ache like a moth - er, twice the price_ of my thrills._ An it's a   cold   day,_ it's a

Rhy. Fig. 1B

Rhy. Fig. 2

(end Rhy. Fig. 2A)

w/Rhy. Figs. 2 & 2A (both 3 times)

con - ti - nen - tal drift._ I said this traf - fic is hell._ Can you   give me a lift?_ An I'll

try to paint_ a sto - ry, got your   pic - tures to tell.   Yeah, you got to make_ a liv - ing with what you

2nd Verse
w/Rhy. Figs. 1 & 1A
A5

bring your - self to sell.   I   got___ some gen - u - ine   im - i - ta - tion bad ap - ples.

w/Rhy. Figs. 2 & 2A (both 2 times)
E5

w/Rhy. Figs. 1A & 1B

Free   sam - ple for your peace o' mind,_ on - ly nine   nine - ty - five.
I   got my cam - 'ra back_ from cus - toms, got my

law fees up to date._ Hell,   they must - a seen_ me com - in'. Ain't this life so fuck - in' great._   When the

103

DON'T CRY (ORIGINAL)

Words and Music by Izzy Stradlin'
and W. Axl Rose

Lead vocal doubled one octave higher (till Guitar solo).

Don't you cry_____ to-night. There's a heav-en a-bove____ you, ba - by.____
Ooh. _____ Ooh.) _____

And don't you cry_____ to-night.

(cont. in slashes)

2nd Verse
w/Fill 2

Give me a whis-per,

Fill 2

Gtr. II

clean tone w/echo
p

*Play only lowest note of chord when P.M.
is indicated (throughout).

Fdbk. pitch.: A

*Vib. applies to bottom note only.

3rd Verse
w/Fill 3

And please   re - mem - ber   that I nev - er___ lied.___

*Lead vocal doubled one octave
higher (next 2 bars).

Don't you cry_ to-night._

THE GARDEN

Words and Music by West Arkeen,
Del James and W. Axl Rose

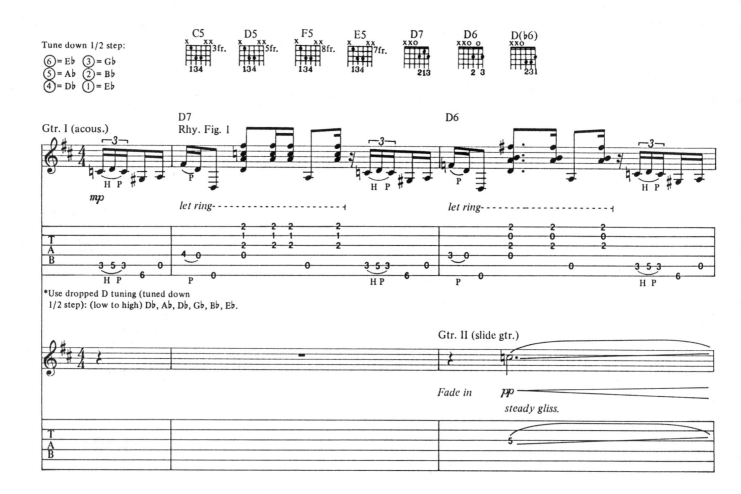

*Use dropped D tuning (tuned down
1/2 step): (low to high) Db, Ab, Db, Gb, Bb, Eb.

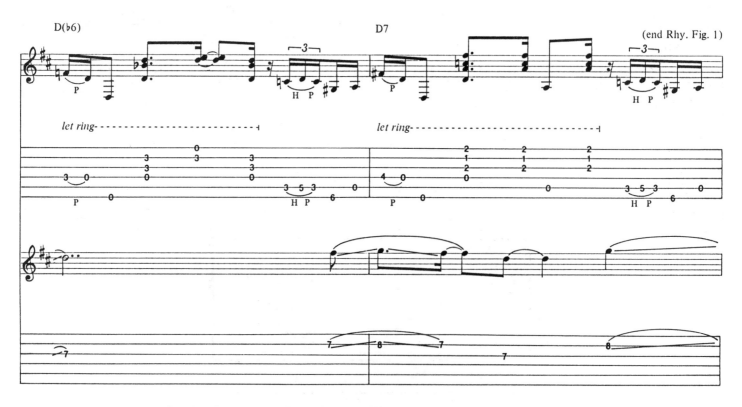

to my worst pho-bi-a, a cra-zy man's_ u-to-pi-a. If you're lost no one can show ya, but it

sure was glad to know ya. On-ly poor boys_ take a chance_ on the gar-den's song and dance._ Feel her

flow-ers as they wrap a-round,_ but on-ly smart boys do with-out.

Ah._____
Ah._____

Ah._____
Ah._____

*Don't pick.

Fdbk. pitch: E

D

on - ly smart boys do with - out. Turned in - to my__ worst pho - bi - a, it's a cra - zy man's__ u - to - pi - a. If you're

lost no one can show ya, but it sure was glad to know__ya. Bye, bye._____ So long._____ Bye,

Riff C

Fill 8

*Strum behind nut.

DEAD HORSE

Words and Music by
W. Axl Rose

(Spoken:) *Then when she said she was gonna like wreck my car, I didn't know what to do.* Woh!____

son of a gun___ and the gun of a son___ that brought back the dev-il in me.___ Woh, but

I ain't quite what you'd call an old___ soul, still

wet be-hind the ears.___ I been a-round this track a cou-ple of times, but now the

dust is start-in' to clear,___ oh___

Tag
w/Rhy. Fig. 1 (Acous. gtr.)

Sick of this life,___ not that you'd care.___

(Band out)

I'm not the on - ly one___ with whom these feel - ings I share.___

CIVIL WAR

(Special Thanks Niven/James)

Words and Music by
Slash, Duff McKagan
and W. Axl Rose

*Recitation: "What we've got here is... failure to communicate. Some men you just can't reach, so you get what
we had here last week, which is the way he wants it. Well, he gets it! N' I don't like it any more than you men."*

138

his - t'ry hides the lies__ of our civ - il wars.__

D'you wear a black arm - band__ when they shot the man__ who said,

Rhy. Fill 2

Rhy. Fill 3

144

car - ry the cross___ of hom - i - cide.___ And his - t'ry bears the scars___ of our civ - il wars.___

*Recitation: "We practice selective annihilation of mayors and government officials. For example, to create a vacuum. Then we fill that vacuum, as popular war advances. Peace is closer."

145

YESTERDAYS

Words and Music by
West Arkeen, Del James,
Billy McCloud and W. Axl Rose

1st, 2nd, 3rd Verses
w/Rhy. Figs. 1 & 1A
3rd time w/Fill 1

1. Yes - ter - day_____ there was so man - y things_ I was nev - er told._
2.3. See additional lyrics

Now that I'm start - in' to learn,_ I feel I'm grow - in' old._ 'Cause

yes - ter - day's_ got noth- in' for me._ Old pic - tures that I'll al - ways see._

Time just fades the pag - es in my book of mem - o - ries._ all just let them be_

Ooh,_____ yes - ter - day's_____ got noth - in' for me._

*w/distortion

Fill 1 (end of solo)

150

Additional Lyrics

2. Prayers in my pocket
And no hand in destiny.
I'll keep on movin' along
With no time to plant my feet.
'Cause yesterday's got nothin' for me.
Old pictures that I'll always see.
Some things could be better
If we'd all just let them be. *(To Chorus)*

3. Yesterday there were so many things
I was never shown.
Suddenly this time I found
I'm on the streets and I'm all alone.
Yesterday's got nothin' for me.
Old pictures that I'll always see.
I ain't got time to reminisce
Old novelties. *(To Chorus)*

PRETTY TIED UP
(THE PERILS OF ROCK N' ROLL DECADENCE)

Words and Music by
Izzy Stradlin'

you she's the right one. Oh no, oh no, oh no.

I can't tell___ you she's___ the right___ one.

158

Additional Lyrics

2. Once there was this rock n' roll band rollin' on the streets.
   Time went by and it became a joke.
   We just needed more and more fulfilling—uh-huh.
   Time went by and it all went up in smoke.
   But check it out. *(To Chorus)*

3. Once you made that money, it costs more now.
   It might cost a lot more than you'd think.
   I just found a million dollars that someone forgot.
   It's days like this that push me o'er the brinks.
   *Cool and stressing. *(To Chorus)*

   **Pronounced "Kool Ranch Dres'ing"*

LOCOMOTIVE (COMPLICITY)

Words and Music by
Slash and W. Axl Rose

161

you won't take the love_ I have to give?____   I___ bought me an il - lu - sion an I

put it   on   the wall._   I   let it   fill___ my head with dreams_ and I had_

___ to have_ them all._   But oh,___ the taste is nev-er so sweet as what you be-lieve it is,___ well I guess___

164

it nev - er is.___ It's these prej - u - diced_ il - lu - sions that pump the blood_ to the heart of the biz.___

how can I for-get you, or try not to re-ject you, when we both know it takes time to for-give,

N.C.(D5)

G5

yeah.

(Gtr. IV out)

Gtrs. I & II

Fill 1 (Gtr. III)

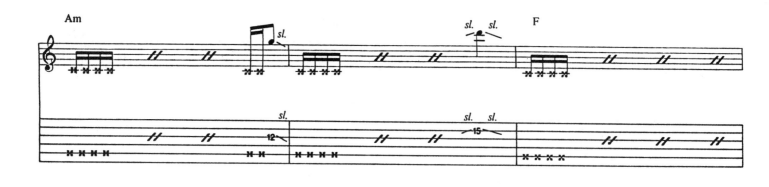

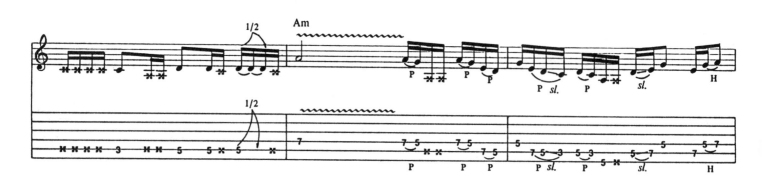

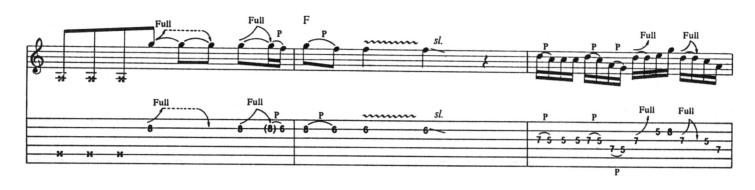

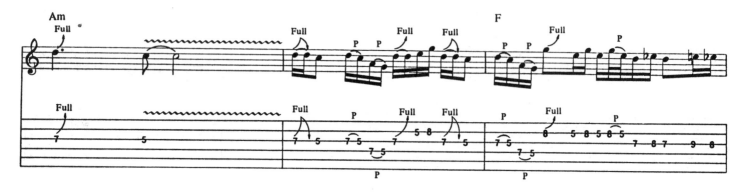

174

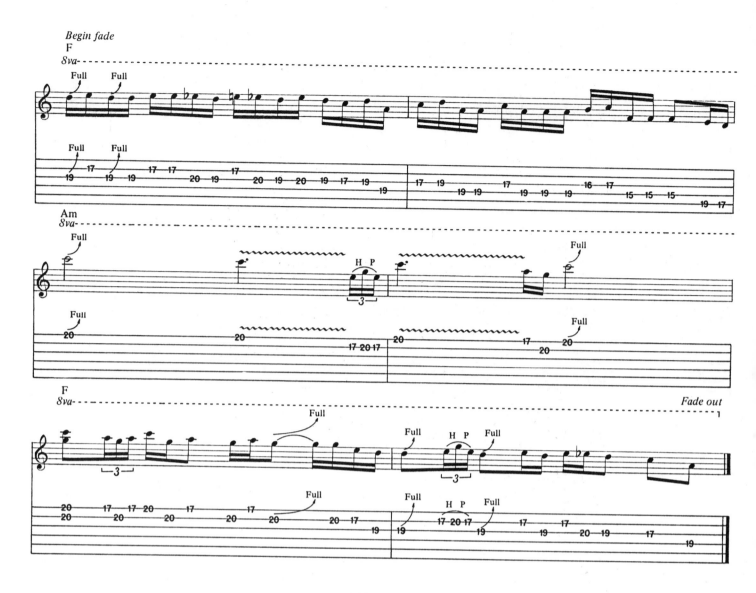

Additional Lyrics

3. Gonna have some with my frustration.
   Gonna watch the big screen in my head.
   I'd rather take a detour 'cause this road ain't gettin' clearer.
   Your train of thought has cut me off again.
   Better tame that boy 'cause he's a wild one,
   Better tame that boy for he's a man.
   Sweetheart, don't make me laugh, you's gettin' too big for your pants,
   And I's think maybe you should cut out while you can.
   You can use your illusion, let it take you where it may.
   We live and learn, and then sometimes it's best to walk away.
   Me, I'm just here hangin' on,
   It's my only place to stay, at least for now anyway.
   I've worked too hard for my illusions just to throw them all away. *(To Interlude III)*

4. I'm taking time for quiet consolation,
   In passing by this love that's passed away.
   I know it's never easy, so why should you believe me
   When I've always got so many things to say?
   Calling off the dogs, a simple choice is made,
   'Cause playful hearts can sometimes be enraged.
   You know I tried to wake you, I mean how long could it take you
   To open up your eyes and turn the page.

2nd Pre-chorus:
Kindness is a treasure and it's one towards me you've seldom shown.
So I'll say it for good measure, to all the one's like you I've known.
Ya know I'd like to shave your head and all my friends could paint it red.
'Cause love to me's a two way street an all I really want is peace. *(To Chorus)*

3rd Pre-chorus:
Affection is a blessing, can you find it in your sordid heart?
I tried to keep this thing ta-gether, but the tremor tore my pad apart.
Yeah, I know it's hard to face when all we've worked.for's gone to waste.
But you're such a stupid woman and I'm such a stupid man, but love like time's got it's own plans. *(To Chorus)*

ESTRANGED

Words and Music by
W. Axl Rose

Tune down 1/2 step:
⑥ = Eb ③ = Gb
⑤ = Ab ② = Bb
④ = Db ① = Eb

Moderately slow ♩ = 89

When you're talk-in' to your-self and no-bod-y's home,

*Some chord names implied by piano.

you can fool your-self. You came in this world a-lone.___ (Whispered:) A-lone.___

So, no-bod-y ev-er told you, ba — by, how it was gon-na be.____

What-'ll hap-pen to_ you, ba — by, guess we'll have to wait_ and

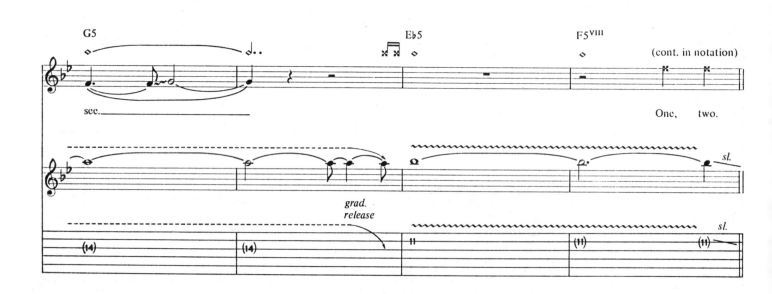

see.____

(cont. in notation)

One, two.

So, what-'ll hap- pen to_ us, ba - by, guess we'll have to wait_ and see.

*Bass in chord names refers to bass gtr. (next 2 bars).

talk so loud,   an you don't walk_ so proud_   an - y - more,   and what for?

Well, I jumped in - to the riv -
(Gtr. II out)

w/Rhy. Fig. 1

er too man - y times_ to make_ it home._ I'm out here_ on my own,_ an drift - ing all_

a - lone._ If it does - n't show,____ give it time_ to read be - tween the lines.____

'Cause I see the storm is get - ting clos - er,_____

187

*Gtr. IV indicated to right of slash in tab.

*Piano arr. for gtr.

YOU COULD BE MINE

(Special Thanks To Bernie Taupin and Elton John)

Words and Music by Izzy Stradlin'
and W. Axl Rose

194

1. I'm a cold heart-break-er, fit ta burn, and I'll rip your heart in two,

2. *See additional lyrics*

and I'll leave you ly-in' on the bed.

You could be mine.

You could be mine. *(Whispered:)* Sh -sh -sh -sh - sh. You could be mine.

You could be mine. Sh -sh -sh -sh. You could be mine, mine, mine, mine!

Ooh, you've gone sketch-in' too man-y times. Woo,

why don't ya give it a rest. Why

must you find

an - oth - er rea - son to cry?

While you're break-in' down my back n' I been rack-in' out my brain, it don't
(Gtr. III out)

Additional Lyrics

2. Now, holidays come, and then they go,
   It's nothin' new today,
   Collect another memory.
   When I come home late at night,
   Don't ask me where I've been.
   Just count your stars I'm home again. *(To Chorus)*

TABLATURE: A six-line staff that graphically represents the guitar fingerboard. By placing a number on the appropriate line, the string and fret of any note can be indicated. For example:

| 1st string - High E |
| 2nd string - B |
| 3rd string - G |
| 4th string - D |
| 5th string - A |
| 6th string - Low E |

5th string, 3rd fret   2nd string, 10th fret and 3rd string, 9th fret played together   an open E chord

Definitions for Special Guitar Notation

BEND: Strike the note and bend up ½ step (one fret).

BEND: Strike the note and bend up a whole step (two frets).

BEND AND RELEASE: Strike the note and bend ½ (or whole) step, then release the bend back to the original note. All three notes are tied; only the first note is struck.

PRE-BEND: Bend the note up ½ (or whole) step, then strike it.

PRE-BEND AND RELEASE: Bend the note up ½ (or whole) step, strike it and release the bend back to the original note.

UNISON BEND: Strike the two notes simultaneously and bend the lower note to the pitch of the higher.

VIBRATO: Vibrate the note by rapidly bending and releasing the string with a left-hand finger.

WIDE OR EXAGGERATED VIBRATO: Vibrate the pitch to a greater degree with a left-hand finger or the tremolo bar.

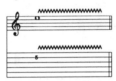

SLIDE: Strike the first note and then with the same left-hand finger move up the string to the second note. The second note is not struck.

SLIDE: Same as above, except the second note is struck.

SLIDE: Slide up to the note indicated from a few frets below.

HAMMER-ON: Strike the first (lower) note, then sound the higher note with another finger by fretting it without picking.

PULL-OFF: Place both fingers on the notes to be sounded. Strike the first (higher) note, then sound the lower note by pulling the finger off the higher note while keeping the lower note fretted.

TRILL: Very rapidly alternate between the note indicated and the small note shown in parentheses by hammering on and pulling off.

TAPPING: Hammer ("tap") the fret indicated with the right-hand index or middle finger and pull off to the note fretted by the left hand.

NATURAL HARMONIC: With a left-hand finger, lightly touch the string over the fret indicated, then strike it. A chime-like sound is produced.

ARTIFICIAL HARMONIC: Fret the note normally and sound the harmonic by adding the right-hand thumb edge or index finger tip to the normal pick attack.

TREMOLO BAR: Drop the note by the number of steps indicated, then return to original pitch.

PALM MUTE: With the right hand, partially mute the note by lightly touching the string just before the bridge.

MUFFLED STRINGS: Lay the left hand across the strings without depressing them to the fret-board; strike the strings with the right hand, producing a percussive sound.

PICK SLIDE: Rub the pick edge down the length of the string to produce a scratchy sound.

TREMOLO PICKING: Pick the note as rapidly and continuously as possible.

RHYTHM SLASHES: Strum chords in rhythm indicated. Use chord voicings found in the fingering diagrams at the top of the first page of the transcription.

SINGLE-NOTE RHYTHM SLASHES: The circled number above the note name indicates which string to play. When successive notes are played on the same string, only the fret numbers are given.

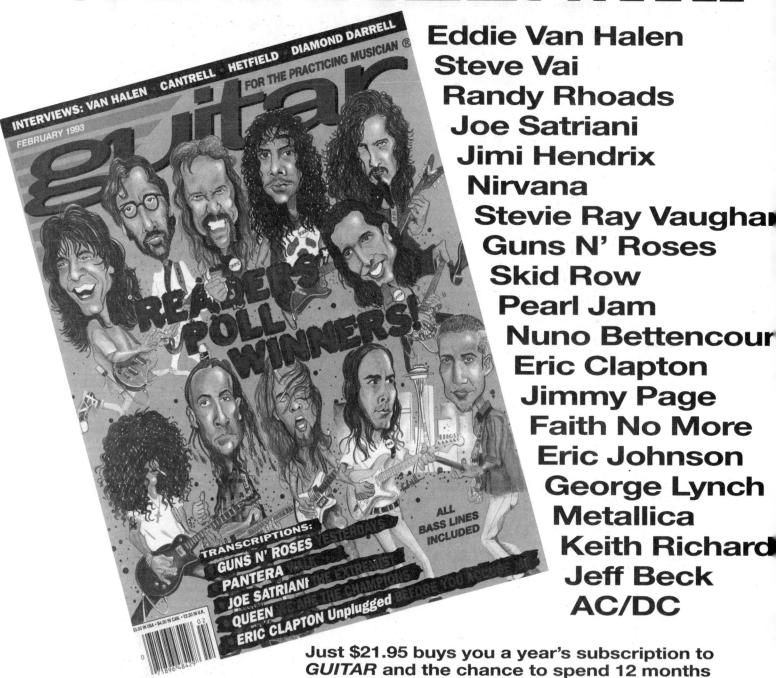